How To

Get Over And Move On

When You Lose Your

Relationship

by

Henrice Kupper

How To

Get Over And Move On

When You Lose Your

Relationship

Table of contents

INTRO 5

FOREWORD 7

LOSS.. 8

SHARING YOUR FEELINGS 11

THE HATE PHASE 15

DEAL WITH IT 16

JOURNALING 20

WRITING IT 21

GET ORGANIZED................................ 23

GET RID OF THINGS THAT BRING

BACK MEMORIES 25

DON'T LAY AROUND.......................... 27

WRAPPING UP 29

ABOUT THE AUTHOR 31

INTRO

Thank for purchase this book. On my website www.deditio.com you can read, view and listen to more valuable information on how to become happy.

Being happy is hard work. Every day again invest in yourself. Learn a lot, try things out and adapt them. Think and refine. Refine again and again until you become a master of happiness. By trial and error, dealing creative with things and let go. Especially let things go ....

Do the things different, seek for possibilities and do not be afraid. Reward yourself and give yourself many compliments to motivate you so you keep going on. Be proud of yourself. Be open to other cultures and opinions. Form your own opinion. Discover how the world works and how you can profit of it. Discover what your place and goal is in your life.

And if you finally know how the world works and know how you can pick the fruits of, than you only need some maintenance and you will live in abundance!

I found mine key to happiness and abundance, how about you?

Take advantage of my knowledge and let me guide you on your journey until you can travel by yourself.

FOREWORD

Breakups may be harsh, and they may be amicable; regardless what, no one truly wants to go through them. The loss of your relationship may bring on acute heartache. However if you're looking for a little help getting through it and want a few suggestions about how to make it a bit easier, read on...

About break-up

If you have just had a break-up and are feeling down, you're not unaccompanied. Just about everybody experiences a break-up at onetime, and several then have to deal with heartbreak — a wave of sorrow, anger, confusion, low self-regard, and perhaps even jealousy all together. 1000000s of poems and songs have been composed about having a cracked heart and wars have even been crusaded because of broken-heartedness.

LOSS

Lots of things may cause heartbreak. A few individuals might have had a romantic relationship that stopped before they were ready. Other people may have strong feelings for somebody who does not feel the same way.

Or perhaps an individual feels sad or angry if a close friend ends or deserts the friendship. While the causes might be different, the sensing of loss is the same — whether it's the loss of something true or the loss of something you only anticipated. Individuals describe brokenheartedness as a feeling of heaviness, emptiness, and sorrow.

Most individuals will tell you you'll get over it or you'll meet somebody else, but when it's happening to you, it may feel as if no one else in the cosmos has ever felt the same way. If you're feeling these feelings, there are things you are able to do to lessen the pain. Here are a few tips that may help and we will look at some of them in more detail in later chapters:

Share your feelings. A few individuals find that sharing their feelings with somebody they trust — somebody who recognizes what they're experiencing — helps them feel better. That may mean talking over all the particulars you feel, even having a great cry on the shoulder of a consolatory acquaintance or family member.

Other people find they heal better if they hang out and do the things they generally love, like seeing a film or going to a concert, to take their brains off the hurt. If you feel like somebody can't tie in to what you're experiencing or is dismissive of your feelings, find somebody more sympathetic to talk to. Talk with an acquaintance or loved ones, a teacher, or counselor.

Remember what's great about you. This one is truly crucial. Sometimes individuals with broken hearts begin to blame themselves for what's occurred. They might be really down on themselves, exaggerating their flaws as if they did something to merit the unhappiness they're going through. If you find this occurring, nip it in the bud! Remind yourself of your great qualities, and if you can't think of them because your broken heart is corrupting your view, get your acquaintances to remind you.

Take great care of yourself. A broken heart may be really stressful so don't let the rest of your body get broken as well. Get lots of sleep, eat sound foods, and exercise regularly to downplay stress and depression and give your self-respect a boost.

Don't be frightened to cry. Experiencing a break-up may be really hard, and getting some of those raw emotions out may be a big help. Crying helps you to release the stress and to become balanced again.

Do the things you commonly enjoy. Whether it's seeing a film or going to a concert, do something fun to take your brain off the damaging feelings for a while.

Keep yourself busy. Occasionally this is hard when you're confronting sadness and grief, but it truly helps. This is a good time to redecorate your room or try a fresh hobby. That doesn't mean you should not consider what occurred — working things through in our brains is all part of the healing procedure — it simply means you ought to center on additional things too.

SHARING YOUR FEELINGS

Occasionally the hardest thing about feelings is sharing them with other people. Sharing your feelings helps you if your feelings are great and when they aren't so great. Sharing likewise helps you to get closer to individuals you care about and who care about you.

Centering Your Feelings

You can't tell your friends what's inside if you don't know what's in there yourself. Feelings (which lots of individuals also call "emotions") are the same way. Before you are able to share them with anybody, you have to figure out what feelings you have.

Arriving at a list of your feelings may help. You may do this in your head or by writing it out on a sheet of paper or even by drawing pictures. Is something getting at you? Does it make you sad or furious? Do you feel this emotion only once in a while or do you feel it much of the time?

When you're attempting to figure out your feelings, it may help to remember something that occurred and consider how it made you feel. Then you are able to say, "I feel sad when my friend doesn't talk with me" or "I feel angry when my mate always lets me down." This may help you figure out your own feelings. It likewise gives the individual you're talking with more info about what's bothering you.

The way an individual feels inside is crucial. It may be really hard not to tell anybody that you're feeling sad, worried, or upset. Then, it's simply you and these bad feelings. If you keep feelings locked away inside, it may even make you feel sick!

But if you talk with somebody who cares for you, you'll almost always begin to feel better. Now you're not all alone with your issues or worries. It doesn't mean your issues and worries magically disappear, but at least somebody else knows what's bothering you and may help you discover solutions.

When you know who you are able to talk with, you'll need to pick a time and place to talk. Does it need to be private or not? If you think you'll have trouble stating what's on your mind, write it down on a sheet of paper.

If the individual doesn't understand what you mean at once, attempt explaining it a different way or provide an example of what's concerning you. Is there something you think may be done to make things better? If so, say it.

Some people are more private than others. That means some individuals will feel shyer about sharing their feelings. You don't have to share every feeling you have, but it is important to share feelings when you need help. You don't have to solve every issue on your own. Occasionally you need help. And if you do, talking about your feelings may be the first step toward getting it.

THE HATE PHASE

This is when you wish to simply scream as your rage feels limitless. The sum of anger you feel depends upon how antagonistic the split was, the conditions, and how long it took to make the final break.

You might resent your ex for blowing your time. You might recognize that the break was inevitable (hindsight will bring out clues you failed to observe at the time).

You might even feel a lot of anger toward yourself, however let go of that feeling quick! It's a waste of time and vitality to rip yourself apart over something you no more have the power to alter. There are so many favorable things you may do with your emotions and energy.

While it might feel good to replace your feelings of love toward your ex with hate, this may still lead to ramifications and mixed emotions of love and hate which are never a great thing.

DEAL WITH IT

They say hate can't exist without love. And more frequently than not, hate is heaviest when it comes in the place where love once was.

Knowing how to deal with hate is as easy as comprehending this fact.
It's extremely easy to hate somebody, say, your ex's new lady friend, or your best friend's beau who's taking her away from you!

But it is not constantly love lost that leads to hatred. Years of accumulated frustration and neglect as well may make you begin hating somebody. So is jealousy.

There are several who wind up without knowing how to deal with hatred in their hearts, for their siblings, for their onetime friends, mates, or co-workers, as they were ate up by jealousy. Or because they feel what was truly theirs went to the other individual.

However, hate need not always be because of somebody else. It's as much an indicator of your own personality, state psychologists.

If you're among those who are commonly unhappy and dissatisfied with life, it's more likely that you'll have a difficult time dealing with hatred and anger.

If you've constantly thought that you got a raw deal, then in all likelihood, you'll likewise hate the individuals who you believe got it easy. It may be a result of what you experienced in your life. Your past experiences shape what you are now. And all this will only make it more difficult for you to deal with people you hate.

There are individuals who generalize their feelings, for or because of, one person in a whole group. If you had a scornful father, you might subconsciously detest all older men. Or the reason you detest your boss so much may be because he reminds you of that unpleasant teacher who used to constantly pick on you, and lose no chance to mortify you in class, for no fault of yours.

The reasons for hating somebody may be various. But that doesn't in any way alter the fact that you have to deal with the individuals you hate all the same. And it is going to hurt no one as much as it injuries you.

The heftiest argument against hatred is that it's pointless. So you detest that witch in your best friend's life. It isn't going to make your best friend ditch her. It's definitely not going to cause her any sleepless nights.

All it will do is make matters uncomfortable between your friend and you. And make you crazy. That you detest somebody or don't know how to deal with hatred is your issue, not theirs!

You may be so busy hating individuals, that you fail to see love and concern coming from a different direction. You might be too involved in managing all that wrath and hate at your ex-boyfriend who dumped you for a different girl, that you can't see your friend, standing next to you all the while, ready and waiting for you to get over the hurt and anger. You must comprehend that patience may run out eventually.

Even the most truehearted friends may give up and walk away, if they see that regardless how much they care for you and love you, you never notice. Learn to deal with individuals you detest.

It may alter the way you feel about yourself and the world.
Therefore make a choice on how you want to feel and want to do with your life.

JOURNALING

Write in a journal or attempt composing poems. The most crucial thing is to be utterly honest and don't edit yourself as you get going.

Among the best results of writing it all down is that occasionally you'll be astonished by a sudden insight that comes to you as you're pouring it all out onto paper.

Patterns might get clearer, and as your grieving starts to lessen, you'll discover it so much easier to comprehend useful life lessons from the entire experience if you've been composing your way through it.

No relationship is ever a loser if you manage to learn something about yourself. Simply since it didn't work out doesn't mean it wasn't an essential part of your journey to being who you're intended to be.

WRITING IT

Whether you're dealing with the finish of a relationship, the death of a relative, a fight with a friend or family member or simply feeling lonely and blue, writing in a journal is a generative way to deal with your feelings. With journaling as an emotional outlet, you'll have a place to air out your thoughts and deal with these hard situations.

- Buy a peculiar journal or notebook that you're drawn to so that you wish to pick it up and begin writing at once.

- Keep your journal totally confidential. Always compose as if no one will ever read your journal, and make certain that no one does by hiding it in a dependable place where no one will discover it.

- Utilize your journal to let out your real thoughts and feelings. If you're mad at somebody, depressed, lonely or sad, compose it. Being true to yourself while journaling aids in the healing process and presents you a sense of relief.

- Compose freely. When placing your thoughts down on paper, compose your thoughts openly as they come to you. It isn't essential to consider what you're going to write before you compose it. Let your instincts and urges guide your writing so that you start coping with your inmost feelings.

- You might be so disciplined to hide your emotions in daily life that you've trouble letting them out in your journal. Play a sad or angry song to evoke your feelings and inspire you to write.

- Whenever you're feeling hard emotions, make time to journal. Frequent journaling helps you to deal with and manage your emotions on a continuous basis letting you feel less stressed and more relieved.

GET ORGANIZED

A breakup may signify a fresh beginning. There-fore, cleaning and orchestrating your personal space will leave you feeling invigorated and prepared for the fresh things to come.

Get It Together

A mess may be overpowering and depressing, and will simply add to your tension level. The added bonus is that staying busy with tidying your space doesn't call for a lot of brain power, but does call for just enough centering to keep you from recycling pain.

Occupying yourself with such chores designed to make your life better and easier will likewise occupy your brain enough to help you through the rest of the pain.

Clean your room, get a few new posters, clean up the icons on your personal computer desk-top. As trivial as cleaning up sounds, it'll make you feel better.

One reason things pile up on counters, tables, and floors is that they've no "home." "Make certain everything lives someplace,". Storing things in the room where they're utilized helps ensure they get put away when you're finished, and commonly it's best to store like items together.

If it's something you utilize frequently, make certain the storage place is simple to access. If you need to reach to a high shelf and pull down a turkey platter just so you'll be able to return a bowl to its 'home,' odds are it's not going to get put away very frequently.

GET RID OF THINGS THAT BRING BACK MEMORIES

There are all sorts of things that remind you of your ex - a song, an aroma, a sound, a place.

Get Rid Of It

When the grieving period has had a little time to process, don't dwell on terrible feelings or memories. There are likely things that are pressing your buttons without your conscious recognition.

Attempt walking around every room in your home with a box and removing items that make your heart ache or your tummy turn. Truly center and look cautiously.

You might recognize that the little blue bird-shaped box sitting on the mantelpiece has become pretty invisible for the last few years, but when you take a witting look at it, you notice that each time you turn toward that corner of the room and it captures your eye, you feel a keen little pain in your solar plexus.

It may work wonders to clean-cut your space of all these triggers. If you have a souvenir, like a watch or piece of jewelry that was given to you by your ex, and it's a re-minder of the great facets of your relationship, there's nothing wrong with maintaining such a thing, but for the time being, attempt putting it away for later, when you've presented yourself a little time and space.

Place these reminders far away from you, such as in a box in a position you'll never go. Out of view, out of mind.

DON'T LAY AROUND

Exercise betters your mood and alleviates depression, and the misdirection will help keep your brain off your state of affairs.

Get Moving

Go running outside, travel to (or join) the gymnasium, or simply go for a walk, perhaps with an acquaintance, and think of releasing the wrath or sadness with each step. If you don't exercise on a regular basis, here are a few ways to motivate yourself to exercise:

Do something little, right now. Going the whole way to the gymnasium, or becoming decked out in your jogging gear, or doing whatsoever it is you feel you ought to be doing plainly appears like too much work. So simply do 10 push-ups or jumping jacks. Simple.

And commonly, it's simply enough to get your heart rate going a little bit, and make you feel like a bit more exercise wouldn't be so foul.

Get midway there. If you wish to go to the gymnasium, but just don't feel like it, at least simply drive yourself to gymnasium, and tell yourself that if you still don't feel like exercising, you'll go home.

Odds are, though, when you're there, you won't feel like driving home. (However if you do, that's all right too. But you likely won't.)

Then tell yourself you'll simply walk on the treadmill for ten minutes, even if your workout routine involves much more. Simply telling yourself to do one more thing, without having to dedicate to anything else, will make things much simpler. And shortly, your endorphins will come in.

WRAPPING UP

Remember provide yourself time. It takes time for sorrow to go away.

Almost everybody thinks they won't feel normal once more, but the human spirit is astonishing — and the broken-heartedness almost always heals after a while.

But how long will that take? That depends upon what caused your grief, how you deal with loss, and how rapidly you tend to get over things.

Getting over a break-up may take a few days to a lot of weeks — and occasionally even months. A few individuals feel that nothing will make them happy once again and resort to alcoholic beverage or drugs.

Other people feel furious and wish to hurt themselves or somebody else. Individuals who drink, do drugs, or cut themselves to shake off the reality of a loss might think they're numbing their pain, but the feeling is solely temporary.

They're not truly dealing with the pain, solely masking it, which makes all their feelings work up inside and prolongs the sadness.

Occasionally the sadness is so deep — or lasts so long — that an individual might need some extra support.

For somebody who isn't beginning to feel better after a few weeks or who carries on to feel depressed, talking to a counselor or therapist may be really helpful. So be patient with yourself, and let the healing start.

ABOUT THE AUTHOR

Henrice Kupper has a mission to contribute to the happiness and wellbeing of other people by sharing her knowledge and skills.

She is born in the Netherlands, married with her husband Fons and she has four fantastic grown up children, three girls (girl and twin girls) and a boy. They all are married and she and Fons have nine beautiful grandchildren now.

In her life Henrice has known many beautiful moments but she has also experienced many heavy periods. Henrice has gone through many trials like diseases, cancer, physical and mental violence, a heavy car accident, the death of her oldest daughter and so on.

At one day she was forced to ask herself:

WHAT DO YOU WANT?

"All right, Henrice said: what do I want? I do not know. I know what I do not want but what I do want? I really have no idea! Besides that, I also do not know where to begin…"

Eventually she solved this answer and Henrice has re-searched for over thirty years looking for how she can become happy.

Because that is what Henrice wanted. She wants to be happy. No annoying things anymore, she wants warmth, compassion, to be loved, abundance and happiness. She wants that everything goes without saying and above all that she got rest, because she was so tired of fighting…

Henrice found her key to happiness and now she see it as her duty to share her knowledge so other people can find their happiness too.

Henrice went back to college and Henrice is now an aca-demic coach and counsellor, author, trainer, mediator and HR-advisor. In her business DEDITIO she treats and supports people with their personal- relationship- and work-related issues. Henrice does her job with love and passion.

To get acquainted with Henrice and her way of working she wrote severals books.

I'm HAPPY, Are You?
ISBN 9781611025873

This bestseller is available as book and ebook in Dutch and English, German and Spanish.

The Road To Happines – Where To Begin?
ISBN 978-1512153668

If you want more information or support about improving your situation check out my website: www.deditio.com or send your email to info@deditio.com.

I love to hear from you!